T0083164

SHALL I COMPARE THEE?

10 Shakespeare settings for mixed voices

Compiled and edited by Bob Chilcott

MUSIC DEPARTMENT

OXFORD
UNIVERSITY PRESS

OXFORD
UNIVERSITY PRESS

Great Clarendon Street, Oxford OX2 6DP,
United Kingdom

Oxford University Press is a department of the University of Oxford.
It furthers the University's objective of excellence in research, scholarship,
and education by publishing worldwide. Oxford is a registered trade mark of
Oxford University Press in the UK and in certain other countries

© Oxford University Press 2015

Bob Chilcott has asserted his right under the Copyright, Designs
and Patents Act, 1988, to be identified as the Editor of this anthology

Each composer has asserted his/her right under the Copyright, Designs and
Patents Act, 1988, to be identified as the Composer/Arranger of their Work(s)

Database right Oxford University Press (maker)

First published 2015

Impression: 1

All rights reserved. No part of this publication may be reproduced,
stored in a retrieval system, or transmitted, in any form or by any means,
without the prior permission in writing of Oxford University Press

Permission to perform the works in this anthology in public
(except in the course of divine worship) should normally be obtained
from the Performing Right Society Ltd (PRS) at www.prsformusic.com
or a local performing right licensing organization, unless the owner or the
occupier of the premises being used already holds a licence from such an
organization. Likewise, permission to make and exploit a recording must
be obtained in advance from the Mechanical-Copyright Protection
Society Ltd (MCPS) at www.prsformusic.com or a local mechanical
copyright licensing organization

Enquiries concerning reproduction outside the scope of the above should be
directed to the Music Rights Department, Oxford University Press, at
music.permissions.uk@oup.com or at the address above

ISBN 978-0-19-340614-8

Music and text origination by
Katie Johnston
Printed in Great Britain on acid-free paper by
Halstan & Co. Ltd, Amersham, Bucks.

Preface

In order to mark the four hundredth anniversary of the death of William Shakespeare, we have collected together ten newly composed settings of some of his most familiar words. Many singers all over the world will be familiar with so many of the songs in Shakespeare's plays through the work of composers such as Ralph Vaughan Williams, Gerald Finzi, Sir Michael Tippett, Frank Martin, and John Rutter, to name but a few. For this collection we have asked composers from Britain, Canada, and Finland to put their own stamp on Shakespeare's songs and texts—words that abound with energy and have so much singing line and rhythm within them; words that, in fact, are in most cases surely meant to be sung.

Our source for the texts, and for general reference, has been The Oxford Shakespeare edition, and we have been extremely lucky to have had guidance from Carol Rutter, Professor of Shakespeare and Performance Studies at Warwick University. I am also grateful to the estate of William Walton for allowing me to make a version for voices of his piece 'Touch her soft lips and part', taken from the 1947 *Two Pieces for Strings from 'Henry V'*. I would also like to thank Philip Croydon, Commissioning Editor at Oxford University Press, for his support and guidance on this book, and also Robyn Elton for her careful editing work.

In putting this collection together, I hope we have achieved our aim of creating a practical performance edition that can be used by choirs everywhere to celebrate the life and work of one of our greatest writers—as well as the music of some wonderful contemporary composers.

Bob Chilcott
June 2015

Also available from Oxford University Press:
Hark, hark, the lark: 8 Shakespeare settings for upper voices (978–0–19–340615–5)

Contents

Come away, come away death 6
Howard Skempton

Fear no more the heat o' th' sun 8
Jussi Chydenius

I know a bank where the wild thyme blows 20
Sarah Quartel

If music be the food of love 26
Richard Allain

It was a lover and his lass 36
Will Todd

Shall I compare thee to a summer's day? 45
Owain Park

Sigh no more, ladies 52
Cecilia McDowall

The Bird of Dawning 62
Bob Chilcott

Touch her soft lips and part 68
William Walton arr. Bob Chilcott

When that I was and a little tiny boy 72
Alan Bullard

Come away, come away death

William Shakespeare
from *Twelfth Night* (Act 2, Scene 4)

HOWARD SKEMPTON
(b. 1947)

Duration: 1.5 mins

© Oxford University Press 2015. Photocopying this copyright material is ILLEGAL.

33
mp
one so true Did share it. Not a flo-wer, not a flo-wer
mp
41
sweet On my black cof-fin let there be strown. Not a friend,
48
not a friend greet My poor corpse, where my bones shall be
56
mf
mp
thrown. A thou-sand thou-sand sighs to save, Lay me O where
mf
mp
63
rit.
Sad true lov-er ne-ver find my grave, To weep there.

for Chamber Choir Cantinovum and Rita Varonen

Fear no more the heat o' th' sun

William Shakespeare
from *Cymbeline* (Act 4, Scene 2)

JUSSI CHYDENIUS
(b. 1972)

Duration: 4.5 mins

© Oxford University Press 2015. Photocopying this copyright material is ILLEGAL.

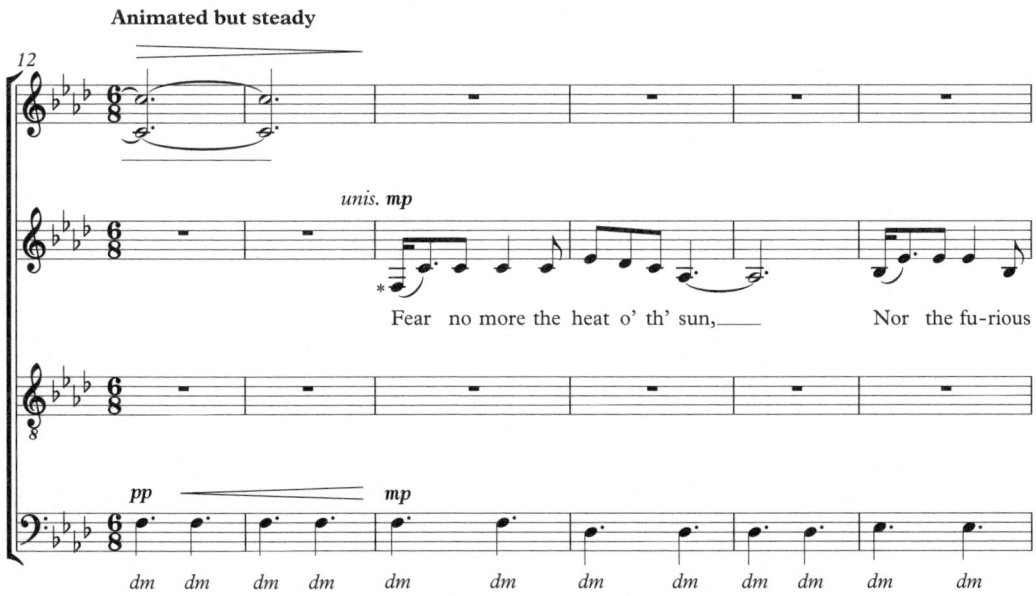

* The alto melody may be doubled by a few tenors, if desired.

18
A.
win - ter's ra - ges.
Thou thy world - ly task hast done,
B.
dm dm dm dm dm dm dm dm dm dm
23
Home art gone and ta'en thy wa - ges.
Gold - en lads and
dm dm dm dm dm dm dm dm
27
come to
div.
girls all must, As chim - ney-sweep - ers,
dm dm dm dm dm dm dm
31
mp
S.
Fear no more the frown o' th' great,
Thou art past the
dust.
oo
p
A.
p
dm dm dm dm dm oo dm dm dm dm
T.
p
dm dm dm dm oo dm dm
B.
p
dm dm dm dm dm dm dm dm dm dm dm dm dm

35
ty - rant's stroke. Care no more to clothe and eat, To
oo
dm dm dm dm oo dm dm dm dm dm oo
dm dm dm dm dm dm dm dm oo
dm dm dm dm dm dm dm dm dm dm dm dm dm dm dm
40
sub. pp
thee the reed is as the oak. The scep - tre, learn - ing,
oo
unis.
sub. pp
dm dm dm dm dm dm dm dm dm dm dm dm scep - tre, learn - ing,
sub. pp
dm dm dm dm dm dm dm dm scep - tre, learn - ing,
sub. pp
dm dm dm dm dm dm dm dm scep - tre, learn - ing,
sub. pp

44
mf
phy-sic, must All fol - low this and...
come to
div. mf
phy-sic, must All fol - low this,
dm dm dm dm dm dm dm
phy-sic, must All fol - low this,
dm dm dm dm dm dm dm
phy-sic, must All fol - low this,
dm dm dm dm dm dm dm
mf
mp
48
mf
Fear no more the light - ning flash,
dust.
mp
d k dm dm d k dm dm ah
mp
d k dm dm d k dm dm ah
mp
dm dm d k dm dm dm d k dm dm dm dm d k dm

51
Nor_ th' all-dread - ed thun - der - stone.
ah
ah
mp
d k dm dm dm d k dm dm dm
ah
d k dm dm d k dm dm d k dm dm
dm dm d k dm dm dm d k dm dm dm d k d k
54
Fear_ not slan - der, cen - sure rash.
d k dm dm d k dm dm ah
d k dm dm d k dm dm ah
dm dm d k dm dm dm d k dm dm dm dm d k dm

57
Thou hast fi-nished joy and moan. All lov - ers young, all
ah
unis.
mf
d k dm dm dm d k dm dm dm dm dm dm dm dm lov - ers young, all
mf
d k dm dm d k dm dm dm dm dm dm lov - ers young, all
mf
dm dm d k dm dm dm d k dm dm dm lov - ers young, all
mf
61
lov-ers must Con - sign to thee and...
f
lov-ers must Con - sign to thee, dm dm dm dm dm dm dm come to
f
mp
lov-ers must Con - sign to thee, dm dm dm dm dm dm dm
f
lov-ers must Con - sign to thee, dm dm dm dm dm dm dm
f
f
mp

65
S.
A.
dust.
pp
sim.
T.
B.
Fear no more, no more, fear no more, fear no more, no more, fear no more,
67
p
sim.
fear no more, no more, fear no more, fear no more, no more, fear no more,
p
No ex - or - ci - zer harm thee,
69
mp
fear no more, no more, fear no more, fear no more, no more, fear no more,
71
mf
S.
Nor no witch - craft charm thee.
mp
div.
A.
fear no more, no more, fear no more, fear no more, no more, fear no more,
mp
T.
B.
fear no more, no more, fear no more, fear no more, no more, fear no more,
mp

73
f
Ghost un - laid for - bear thee.
Ghost un - laid for - bear thee.
mf
fear no more, no more, fear no more, fear no more, no more, fear no more,
mf
fear no more, no more, fear no more, fear no more, no more, fear no more,
mf
75
No-thing ill come near thee.
No-thing ill come near thee.
fear no more, no more, fear no more, fear no more, no more, no more.
fear no more, no more, fear no more, fear no more, no more, no more.

78
rall.
pp
Qui - et con - sum - ma - tion have, And re - nown - ed be thy grave.
pp
Qui - et con - sum - ma - tion have, And re - nown - ed be thy grave.
rall.
pp
Slower ♩. = 46
83
p dolce
S.
Fear no more the heat o' th' sun, Nor the fu - rious
unis. p dolce
A.
Fear no more the heat o' th' sun,
p dolce
T.
Fear no more the heat o' the sun,
p dolce
B.
Fear no more the heat o' the sun,
Slower ♩. = 46
p dolce

accel.
Tempo I (♩. = 56)
87
mp
win - ter's ra - ges.
Thou thy world - ly task hast done,
Thou thy world - ly task hast done,
div.
mp
win - ter's ra - ges.
d k dm dm
d k dm dm
mp
win - ter's ra - ges.
d k dm dm
d k dm dm
mp
win - ter's ra - ges.
dm
dm d k dm dm
dm d k dm
accel.
Tempo I (♩. = 56)
mp
91
Home art gone and ta'en thy wa - ges.
ah
ah
d k dm dm dm
d k dm dm dm
unis.
ah
ah
d k dm dm
d k dm dm
ah
dm dm dm d k dm dm
dm d k dm dm
dm d k dm
ah

Calmly
95
f
pp
Gold - en lads and girls all must, As chim - ney-sweep - ers, come to
Gold - en lads and girls all must, As chim - ney-sweep - ers,
Gold - en lads and girls all must, As chim - ney-sweep - ers,
Gold - en lads and girls all must, As chim - ney-sweep - ers,
Calmly
99
mp
dust. Fear no more.
Fear no more, more, more, no more.
div.
pp
Fear no more, no more, no more, no more.
Fear no more, more, more, no more.
Fear no more, no more, no more, no more.

Commissioned by the Agincourt Singers (James Pinhorn, Conductor)
in celebration of the one hundredth anniversary of the Agincourt Collegiate Institute

I know a bank where the wild thyme blows

William Shakespeare
from *A Midsummer Night's Dream* (Act 2, Scene 1)

SARAH QUARTEL
(b. 1982)

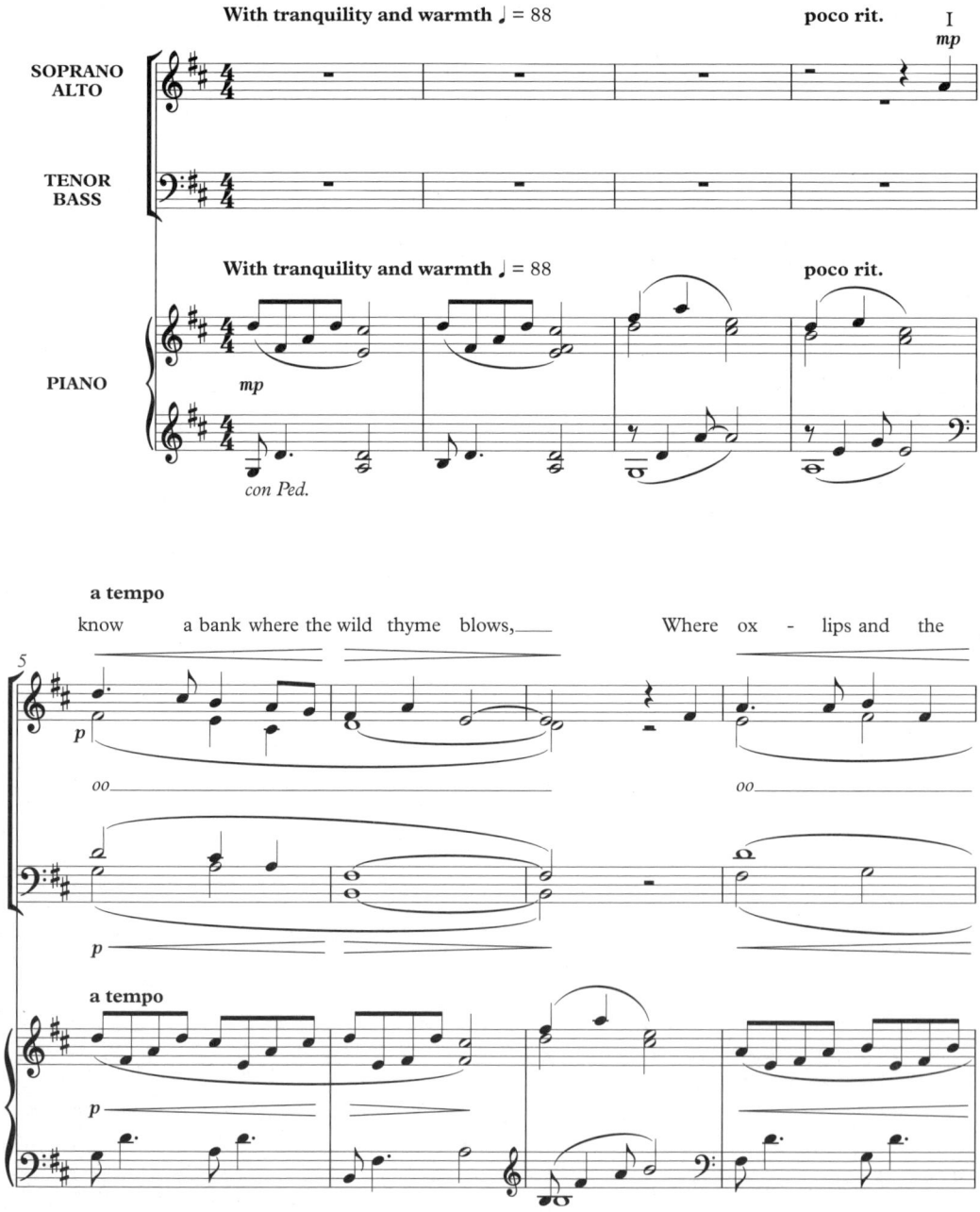

Duration: 3 mins

© Oxford University Press 2015. Photocopying this copyright material is ILLEGAL.

* *eglantine* = sweet briar, a species of wild rose

know a bank where the wild thyme blows.
20
oo
24
mf
There sleeps Ti - tan - ia some-time of the night,
mf
mf legato
28
3
Lulled in these flo - wers with dan-ces and de-light;
f
And
flo - wers

* *throws* = sheds
† *weed* = garments

43
ox - lips and the nod - ding vio - let grows,
mp
46
Quite o - ver - can - o - pied with lus - cious
49
wood - bine, With sweet musk -
mp

52
- ros - es, and with eg - lan - tine.
I
mp
poco rit.
55
mf
mp
know a bank where the wild thyme blows
the
mf
mp
poco rit.
mf
59
rit.
dim.
p
wild thyme blows.
dim.
p
rit.
mp
dim.
p
Ped.

for Ashley, Katie, and Emily

If music be the food of love

William Shakespeare
from *Twelfth Night* (Act 1, Scene 1)

RICHARD ALLAIN
(b. 1965)

Duration: 3.5 mins

© Oxford University Press 2015. Photocopying this copyright material is ILLEGAL.

Poco più mosso ♩ = 96
8
pp
poco a poco cresc.
S.1
Give me ex - cess of it, that sur - feit - ing, The ap - pe -
S.2
Give me ex - cess of it, that sur - feit - ing, The
A.
Give me ex - cess of it, that sur - - feit -
T.
Give me ex - cess of it, that sur - feit - ing,
B.
Give me ex - cess of it, that sur - feit - ing, may
13
f
- tite may sick - en, sick - en and so die.
ap - pe - tite may sick - en and so die.
- ing, sick - en and so die.
The ap - pe - tite may sick - en and so die.
sick - en and so die.

Tempo I (♩ = 88)
18
pp
mf
That strain a - gain, it had a dy - ing fall. O,
That strain a - gain, dy - ing fall.
That strain a - gain, it had a dy - ing fall.
That strain a - gain, it had a dy - ing fall.
That strain a - gain, dy - ing fall.
mp
Tempo I (♩ = 88)
23
Tempo II (♩ = 96)
O, it came o'er my ear like the sweet sound
O, it came like the sweet sound
O, it came like the sound
O'er my ear like the
Sweet
Tempo II (♩ = 96)

27
That breathes, breathes up -
That breathes, breathes up - on
That breathes up-on a bank, up - on a bank,
sweet sound, the sweet sound That breathes up-on, that breathes up - on
sound, up - on,
31
pp
-on a bank, a bank of vio - lets,
a bank, bank of vio - lets,
up - on a bank of vio - lets,
a bank of vio - lets,
up - on a bank of vio - lets,

35
ppp
ff
Steal - ing and giv - ing o - dour. E -
Steal - ing and giv - ing o - dour. E -
Steal - ing and giv - ing o - dour. E -
Steal - ing, giv - ing o - dour. E -
Steal - ing, giv - ing o - dour. E -
39
pp
- nough, no more, 'Tis not so sweet now as it
- nough, no more, 'Tis not so sweet now as it
- nough, no more, 'Tis not so sweet now as it
- nough, no more, not sweet as it
mf
- nough, no more, as it

42
f
mp
was be - fore. Spi - rit of love, how
was be - fore. Spi - rit of love, how quick
was be - fore. O, O
was be - fore. Spi - rit of love, how
was be - fore. O spi - rit of love,
46
quick and fresh art thou, not-with - stand - -
art thou, That not - with - stand - ing thy ca -
how quick and fresh art thou, not - with - stand-
quick and fresh art thou, That not - with - stand -
how fresh art thou, Re - ceiv - eth

50
-ing thy ca - pa - ci - ty Re - ceiv - eth as the
-pa - ci - ty Re - ceiv - eth as the sea,
- ing, Re - ceiv - eth as the sea, naught en - ters there,
-ing thy ca - pa - ci - ty, naught en - ters there,
as the sea, as the
54
f
sea, Of what va - lid - i - ty and pitch so e'er,
sub. f
naught en - ters there, Of what so e'er, But
f
naught en - ters there, But
sub. f
naught en - ters there, there, But
sub. f
sea, Of what va - lid - i - ty and pitch so e'er,
sub. f

59
But falls, but falls,
falls in - to a - bate - ment and low price
falls, falls, but falls,
falls in - to a - bate - ment and low price, but falls,
falls, but falls,
63
p
mp
E - ven in a min - ute! So full of
E - ven in a min - ute! full of
E - ven in a min - - ute! full of
E - ven in a min - - ute! full of
full of

68
mf
shapes That
shapes That it a - lone is
shapes is fan - cy, That it a - lone, that it a -
shapes is fan - cy, it a - lone is
shapes is fan - cy,
72
f
it a - lone is high
high, is high, high, is
- lone, a - lone, that it a - lone is high fan - tas -
high, is high fan - tas - ti - cal, is
That it a - lone is high fan - tas -
it a - lone is

76
fan - - tas - ti - cal, high fan -
fan - tas - ti - cal, is high,
- ti - cal, is high fan - tas - ti - -
fan - tas - ti - cal, is high, is
- ti - cal, fan - - tas - ti - cal,
high fan - tas - ti - - - -
80
meno mosso
mp
-tas - ti - cal.
high fan - - tas - ti - - cal.
-cal, fan - tas - - - ti - cal.
high fan - - tas - ti - - cal.
-cal, fan - tas - - ti - cal.
meno mosso
mp

Commissioned by Mavis Fletcher on behalf of seven choirs as part of ABCD's Auction 2013 (Cantoris, Carleton Community Chorus, Dorking Camerata, Heyhouses Community Choir, Lancaster Singers, Southport Bach Choir, and The Maia Singers)

It was a lover and his lass

William Shakespeare
from *As You Like It* (Act 5, Scene 3)

WILL TODD
(b. 1970)

Duration: 3.5 mins

© Oxford University Press 2015. Photocopying this copyright material is ILLEGAL.

13
cresc.
In
That o'er the green corn-field did pass In
cresc.
17
mf
ring - time,
spring - time, spring - time, the on - ly pret - ty ring - time,
mf
21
When birds do sing, hey
f
f
sing, ding - a - ding ding,
f
rit.
25
p
Sweet lov - ers love the
ding - a - ding ding, Sweet lov - ers love the
pp

29
a tempo
S.
A.
spring.
unis. mp
T./B.
Be-tween the a-cres of the rye,
a tempo
p
mp
p
mp
33
p
Hey, hey - non-ny-no,
With a hey, and a ho, and a hey - - non-ny-no,
p sim.
37
cresc.
Folks would lie,
lie,
In
These pret-ty coun - try folks would lie,
cresc.
In
cresc.

41
mf
spring - time, spring - time, the on - ly pret - ty
mf
spring - time,
mf
44
When birds do sing, hey
f
ring - time, When birds do sing,
f
sing,
f
47
p
ding - a - ding ding, ding - a - ding ding,
ding ding ding,
mp
p
ding,
pp

rit.
a tempo
51
Sweet lov - ers love the spring.
Sweet lov - ers love the spring.
p
ah love spring.
rit.
a tempo
How
55
mf
This ca - rol they be-gan that hour,
How,
How
mf
How,
mf
life was but a flow'r, a
rit.
59
f
how that a life was but, life was but a
life was but a flow'r, a
f
how that a life was but a
f
rit.

a tempo
flow'r.
63
p
flow'r,
flo - - wer.
p
flow'r, a
a tempo
p
66
mf
f
time,
And there-fore take the pre - sent time,
unis.
mf
f
f
And there-fore take the pre - sent time,
69
With a hey, and a ho,

* *prime* = the springtime of life/spring/the height of perfection

83
When birds do sing, hey
When birds do sing,
ding - a - ding ding,
ding ding ding,
mp
When birds do sing,
ding,
87
p
Sweet lov - ers
p
ding - a - ding ding,
Lov - ers love the
Sweet love
p
p
mp p
ding,
ah
p
rit.
91
sweet lov - ers love the
spring,
sweet lov - ers love the
spring,
ah love
rit.

95
a tempo
spring,
ding - a - ding ding,
ding,
mp
p
spring,
mp
ding,
a tempo
p
mp
pp
99
sweet lov - ers
rit.
lov - ers love the
spring,
sweet love
p
ah
spring,
rit.
slower
rit.
103
sweet lov - ers love the spring.
sweet lov - ers love the spring.
ah love spring.
slower
rit.
8va
p
pp

Shall I compare thee to a summer's day?

William Shakespeare
Sonnet 18

OWAIN PARK
(b. 1993)

Duration: 4 mins

© Oxford University Press 2015. Photocopying this copyright material is ILLEGAL.

18
Thou art more love-ly and more tem - per-ate:
22
mf
mp
Rough winds do shake the dar - ling buds of May, And
mf
mp
25
sum-mer's lease hath all too short a date;
p
p
mp en dehors
p
29
S.
A.
p intense
Some-time too hot the eye of hea-ven
T.
B.
p intense
pp

33
mf
mp
shines,
And of - ten is his gold com-ple-xion
mf
mp
mp
sub. p
molto
mf
36
f
dimmed,
And ev-'ry fair from fair some-time de-clines,
f
And ev - 'ry fair from fair some-time de-clines,
f
39
mp
mf
chang-ing
mp
By chance or na - ture's chang-ing, chang - ing, chang-ing
p
mp
mp
By chance, chang - ing, chang-ing
mp

* seamless change to *ah*

52
Nor lose pos-ses-sion of that fair thou ow'st; Nor shall Death brag thou
ah Nor shall Death
Nor lose pos-ses-sion of that fair thou ow'st; Nor shall Death brag thou
ah Nor shall Death
55
wan-der-est in his shade, When in e-ter-nal lines to time thou
brag, When in e-ter-nal...
wan-der-est in his shade, When in e-ter-nal...
brag, When in e-ter-nal...

59
p
grow'st.
p
63
pp (distantly)
mm
p
So long lives this, and
pp (distantly)
mm
p
So long as men can breathe or eyes can see,
p
and
p
So long as men can breathe or eyes can see,
pp
mm

67
this gives life to thee.
this gives life to thee.
meno p
71
rall.
rall.
mp
p
Ped.

Sigh no more, ladies

William Shakespeare
from *Much Ado About Nothing* (Act 2, Scene 3)

CECILIA McDOWALL
(b. 1951)

Duration: 3 mins

© Oxford University Press 2015. Photocopying this copyright material is ILLEGAL.

7
mf
One foot in sea, and one on shore,
One foot in sea, and one on shore,
ev - er, Sigh, sigh, sigh,
ev - er, Sigh, sigh, sigh,
10
To one thing con - stant, con-stant ne-ver, ne-ver,
To one thing con - stant, con - stant ne-ver, ne-ver,
sigh no more, la-dies, sigh, sigh, sigh,
sigh, sigh, sigh,

13
ne-ver, ne-ver, ne - ver.
ne-ver, ne-ver, ne - ver.
sigh, sigh.
sigh, sigh.
16
mp espress.
Sigh no more, la - dies, sigh no more. Men were de-ceiv - ers
mp espress.
Sigh no more, la - dies, sigh no more. Men were de-ceiv - ers
mp dolce

19
mf
ev - er, One foot in sea, and one on shore,
mf
ev - er, ev - er, One foot in sea, and one on shore,
mf
Sigh, sigh, sigh,
mf
Sigh, sigh, sigh,
mf
22
mf
To one thing con - stant, con-stant ne-ver, ne-ver,
mf
To one thing con - stant, con - stant ne-ver, ne-ver,
mf
sigh no more, la-dies, sigh, sigh, sigh,
mf
sigh, sigh, sigh,
mf

25
ne-ver, ne-ver, ne - ver.
ne-ver, ne-ver, ne - ver.
sigh, sigh.
sigh, sigh.
28
mf
cresc.
Then sigh not so, And be you blithe, Con-vert-ing all
Then sigh not so, but let them go, And bon - ny, all,
Then sigh not so, but let them go, go, And be you blithe and
Then sigh not so, but let them go, And be you blithe and

31
f
your sounds of woe, sounds of woe, sounds of
all your sounds of woe, your sounds of
bon - ny, all your sounds of woe, your sounds of
bon - ny, your sounds of woe, your sounds of
35
dim.
pochiss. rit.
p dolce
woe In - to hey non - ny, non - ny.
mf
woe In - to hey non - ny, non - ny, non - ny, non - ny.
woe In - to hey non - ny, non - ny.
woe In - to hey non - ny, non - ny.
mp

a tempo
38
mp
Sing, sing, sing,
mp
Sing no more dit - ties, sing no more Of dumps so dull and
mp
Sing no more dit - ties, sing no more Of dumps so dull and
mp
Sing no more dit - ties, sing no more Of dumps so dull and
a tempo
p dolce
41
mf
sing, sing,
mf
hea - vy, hea - vy. The fraud of men was ev - er so
mf
hea - vy. Sing, sing, sing,
mf
hea - vy. Sing, sing, sing,
mf

44
f
mf
sing,
leaf - y,
Since sum - mer first was leaf - y, leaf - y, leaf - y,
was ev - er so, ev - er so,
leaf - y, leaf - y,
sing, sing, sing,
47
leaf - y, leaf - y, lea - fy, leaf - y.
leaf - y, leaf - y, leaf - y.
was ev - er so.
sing, sing.

50
mf
cresc.
Then sigh not so, And be you blithe, Con-vert-ing all
Then sigh not so, but let them go, And bon - ny, all,
Then sigh not so, but let them go, go, And be you blithe and
Then sigh not so, but let them go, And be you blithe and
53
f
your sounds of woe, sounds of woe,
all your sounds of woe, your
bon - ny, all your sounds of woe, your
bon - ny, your sounds of woe, your

56
dim.
sounds of woe In - to
mf dim.
sounds of woe In - to hey non - ny,
mf dim.
sounds of woe In - to hey non - ny,
mf dim.
sounds of woe In - to hey non - ny,
dim.
59
mp dolce
poco rit.
f
hey non - ny, non - ny, hey non - ny, non - ny no.
mp dolce
f
non - ny, non - ny, non - ny, hey non - ny, non - ny, non - ny, non - ny no.
mp dolce
f
non - ny, hey non - ny, non - ny no.
mp dolce
f
non - ny, in - to hey non - ny, non - ny no.
poco rit.
mf
f

Commissioned by Professor Dame Jessica Rawson
for the Choir of Merton College, Oxford, as part of the Merton Choirbook

The Bird of Dawning

William Shakespeare
from *Hamlet* (Act 1, Scene 1)

BOB CHILCOTT
(b. 1955)

Duration: 2.5 mins

* *'gainst* = towards the time when

© Oxford University Press 2015. Photocopying this copyright material is ILLEGAL.

5
mp dolce
pp
Sa - viour's birth is ce - le - bra - ted, The
mp dolce
pp
Sa - viour's birth is ce - le - bra - ted, The
mp dolce
pp
Sa - viour's birth is ce - le - bra - ted, The
mp dolce
pp
Sa - viour's birth is ce - le - bra - ted, The
mp dolce
pp
SOPRANO SOLO
8
pp
cresc.
ah
ah
S.
cresc.
bird of dawn-ing sing-eth all night long, the bird of dawn-ing sing-eth
A.
cresc.
bird of dawn-ing sing-eth all night long, the bird of dawn-ing sing-eth
T.
cresc.
bird of dawn - ing sing - eth all night,
B.
cresc.
bird of dawn - ing sing - eth all night,
cresc.

11
mf
ah
mf
all night long; And then, they say, and then, and then, they
mf
all night long; And then, they say, and then, and then, and
mf
all night long; And then, they say, and then, and then, and
And then, they say, and then,
mf
unis.
all night long; And then, and then, and
mf
14
dim.
pp
ah
dim.
pp
say, no spi - rit dare stir a -
dim.
pp
then, they say, no spi - rit dare stir a -
dim.
pp
then, they say, no spi - - rit
dim.
pp
then, they say, no spi - - rit
dim.
pp

17
-broad, no spi - rit dare stir, stir a-broad, The
-broad, no spi - rit dare stir, stir a-broad, The
dare stir a - broad, dare stir a-broad, The
dare stir a - broad, a - broad, The
20
mp dolce
ah
mp dolce
nights are whole - some, nights are whole - some,
mp dolce
nights are whole - some, nights are whole - some,
mp dolce
nights are whole - some, nights are whole - some are
mp dolce
nights are whole - some, nights are whole - some, are
mp dolce

* *takes* = bewitches

29
ah
So hal - low'd and so gra - cious is the
gra - cious is the time, is the
gra - cious, hal - low'd is the
gra - cious, hal - low'd is the
32
rit.
pp
time, the time.
time, the time.
pp div.
time.
time, time.
time, time.
rit.
pp

Touch her soft lips and part

William Shakespeare
from *Henry V* (Act 2, Scene 3)*

WILLIAM WALTON (1902–83)
arr. BOB CHILCOTT (b. 1955)

Duration: 1.5 mins

* The words 'Touch her soft lips and part' were adapted from Shakespeare's 'Touch her soft mouth, and march' for the 1944 film of *Henry V*, for which Walton composed the music.

First published in its original version for string orchestra in *Two Pieces for Strings from 'Henry V'* © Oxford University Press 1947. This arrangement © Oxford University Press 2015. Photocopying this copyright material is ILLEGAL.

13
cresc.
me thy lips. Come a - way, come, come, let's a - way. My
me, give me thy lips. Come, come a - way. My
me thy lips. Come, come a - way, come a -
me thy lips. Come, come a - way, come a -
19
mf
p
love, my love, give me thy lips. Come, come a -
unis.
love, my love, give me thy lips, a -
- way. My love, give me thy lips. Come, come a -
- way, give me thy lips. Come a -

24
-way, come, come, let's a - way. My love, my love, give
-way, come, come a - way. My love, my love,
-way, come, come a - way. My love, my love, give
-way, come a - way. My love, my love,
poco rit.
ten.
29
me thy lips, my love, my love, give me thy
give me thy lips, my love, love.
me thy lips, my love, my love, my
unis.
give me thy lips, my love, my
poco rit.
ten.

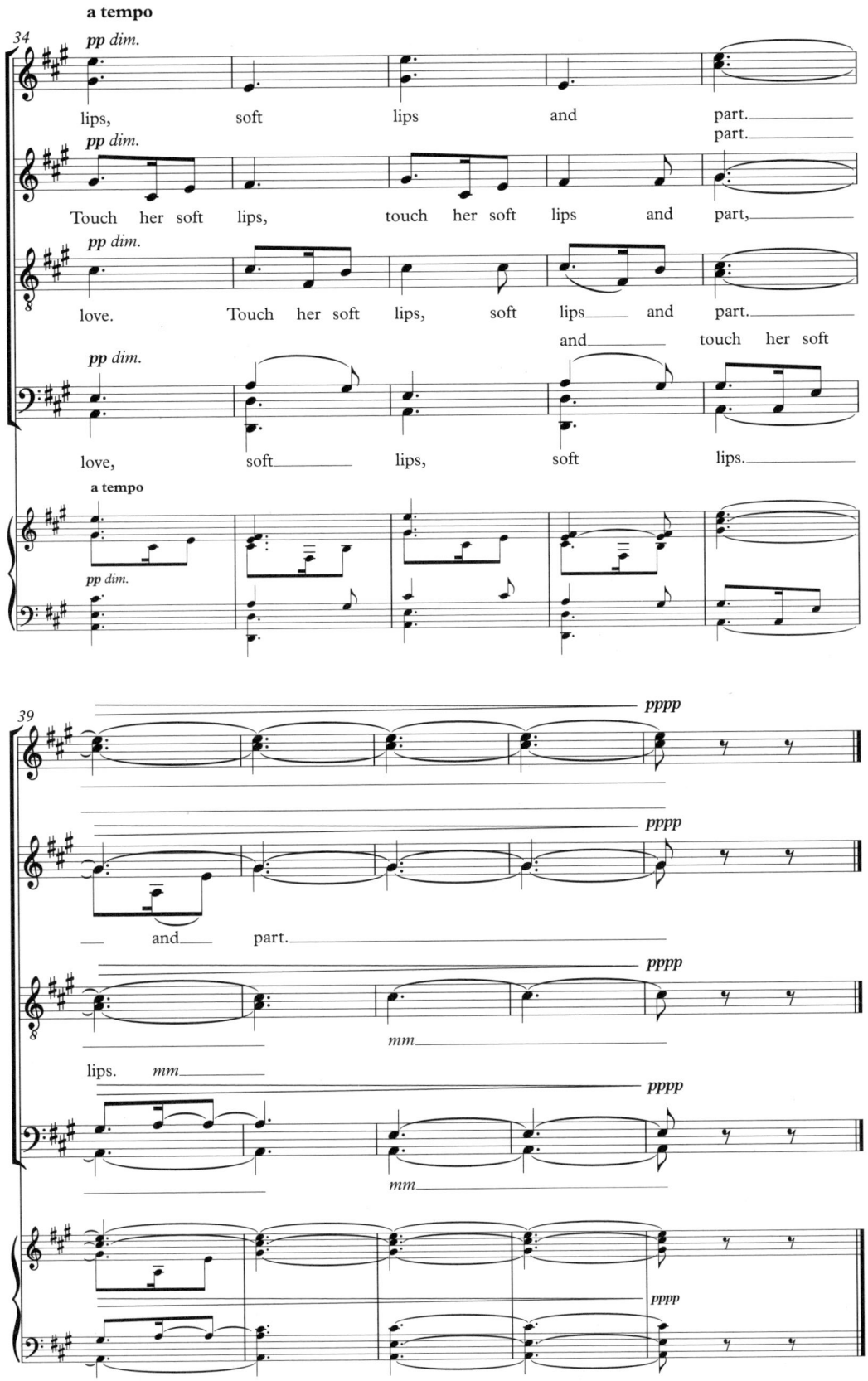
a tempo
34
pp dim.
lips, soft lips and part.
part.
Touch her soft lips, touch her soft lips and part,
love. Touch her soft lips, soft lips and part.
and touch her soft
love, soft lips, soft lips.
39
pppp
and part.
mm
lips. mm

When that I was and a little tiny boy

William Shakespeare
from *Twelfth Night* (Act 5, Scene 1)

ALAN BULLARD
(b. 1947)

Duration: 2.5 mins

* *and a* = just a

© Oxford University Press 2015. Photocopying this copyright material is ILLEGAL.

7
p
mp
rain,
For the rain it rain -
A fool - ish thing was but a toy,
For the rain, the rain it
p
10
- eth ev - 'ry day.
mp
rain - eth ev - 'ry day.
mp
p
Same tempo, but a little more cheerfully
13
f
hey, ho, the
2. But when I came to man's es - tate,
With
hey, ho, hey, the
f
hey, ho, the
Same tempo, but a little more cheerfully
f

16
mf
wind and the rain, 'Gainst knaves and thieves men
wind and the rain,
mf
mf
18
f
p
shut their gate, For the rain, the rain it
p
f
For the rain it
f
p
20
mf
rain - eth ev - 'ry day.
mf
rain - eth ev - 'ry day.
mf

* *swaggering* = blustering, bullying

30
f
rit.
rain it rain - - eth ev - 'ry day.
f
rain, the rain it rain - eth ev - 'ry day.
rit.
mf
f

33
molto rit.
Slower, sleepily ♩ = 88
pp
molto legato
With
(opt. SOLO)
p
(TUTTI)
pp
molto legato
4.But when I came un - to my beds,
molto rit.
Slower, sleepily ♩ = 88
p

* *tosspots* = drunkards

rit.
Subito tempo I, with life (♩ = 126)
43
mp
unis.
p
rain - eth ev - 'ry day.
p
- - eth ev - 'ry day.
rit.
Subito tempo I, with life (♩ = 126)
mp
p
46
f
5. A great while a - go the world be - gun, With
f
f

49
mf
hey, ho, the
wind and the rain,
But that's all one, our
hey, ho, hey, the
hey, ho, the wind and the rain,
mf
mf
52
f
ff
mf
poco a poco accel.
cresc.
play is done,
And we'll strive to please you,
f
ff
mf
cresc.
poco a poco accel.
f
ff
mf
cresc.

55
f
ff
strive to please you ev - - - - 'ry, ev - 'ry
f
ff
f
ff
58
fff
(shout ad lib.)
day,
ev - 'ry day!
(shout ad lib.)
fff
fff